Consider the Possibilities

Pursuing What Matters Most

The Journey

THIS JOURNAL BELONGS TO:

____

____

____

Introduction

I hope by now you have read, **"Consider The Possibilities: Pursuing What Matters Most."** If so, you know about **"The Big It"**. Acknowledging and facing **"The Big It"** is how this journal-coaching process starts. The opening exercise requires you to journal about your **"Big It"**. Remember what happened and how it felt to you. Here are some questions to consider in that first exercise:

- What things did **The Big It** say about you to you?

- What did **The Big It** say about your possibilities for a fulfilling life and the achievement of your life's goals?

- Do you agree with **The Big It's** outlook or can you see new possibilities for your life?

And then we're going to dismantle those reasons week by week. The Possibilities Journal has two goals:

- To intentionally dismantle negative mindsets created by **The Big It**.

- To put the lessons learned during and after **The Big It** to use.

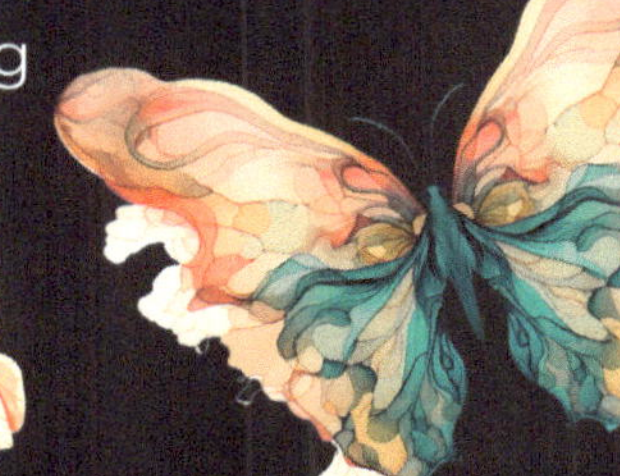

Set your first quarter goals and journey each week towards that goal with smaller tasks, reflections on how you use your words, gratitude, and opportunities to grow. I suggest using this **"journey"** as part of your devotional or meditation time.

Enjoy the journey!

Exercise 1
The Big It: What Happened?

Write about The Big It. (See Chapter 2) Describe the event in as much detail as you think is important. If the timing of The Big It is important, include dates and events that were happening around The Big It (for example, did IT happen during a holiday or around a birthday). What people were involved or around you? Include the details that are important to you.

____

____

____

____

____

____

____

____

____

____

____

____

____

____

Exercise 2
What Changed Inside Me?

Describe the effect of The Big It on you. What changed in how you perceived yourself? What words expressed you before The Big It, and you after? What changed in your relationships with others because of The Big It? How did those changed relationships affect who you thought yourself to be?

____

____

____

____

____

____

____

____

____

____

____

____

____

____

Exercise 3
Where I Want to Go?

Where do I want to go? Take a deep breath. At the end of your life, what would a headline say about your achievements if you pursued them? List the strengths, skills and supporting characters you already have to make the journey. (See Chapter 8) Identify other resources or support that you need.

At the end of my life I want my headline to read:

____

____

____

____

____

____

My Strengths & Abilities

____

____

____

____

____

____

My Support & Accountability People

What Training or Resources Do I Need?

Goals Tracker

My Top Goal(s) For This Quarter

1	
2	
3	

To Do List

Action Plan

STEP 5

STEP 4

STEP 3

STEP 2

STEP 1

Rewards	1	2	3	4

Month 1: ________________

What goal will I set for this month?

____

____

____

____

____

____

____

What words or mindsets might hinder me from meeting my goal?

____

____

____

____

____

____

____

How will I "rewrite the script" to reflect new words and mindsets?

Scripture or Quote and Prayer Target:

I'm grateful for:

____

____

____

____

I'm challenged by:

____

____

____

____

Action Steps

○

○

○

Reflections On This Month

My Accomplishments This Month:

____

____

____

____

____

Where Did I Fall Short In Meeting A Challenge?

____

____

____

____

What Adjustments Can I Make to Move Forward?

____

____

____

____

Month 2: _______________

What goal will I set for this month?

____

____

____

____

____

____

What words or mindsets might hinder me from meeting my goal?

____

____

____

____

____

____

____

How will I "rewrite the script" to reflect new words and mindsets?

____

____

____

____

____

____

Scripture or Quote to Meditate On or Consider

I'm grateful for:

____

____

____

____

I'm challenged by:

____

____

____

____

Action Steps

○

○

○

Reflections On This Month

My Accomplishments This Month:

____

____

____

____

____

Where Did I Fall Short In Meeting A Challenge?

____

____

____

____

____

What Adjustments Can I Make to Move Forward?

____

____

____

____

____

Month 3: _______________

What goal will I set for this month?

____

____

____

____

____

____

____

What words or mindsets might hinder me from meeting my goal?

____

____

____

____

____

____

____

How will I "rewrite the script" to reflect new words and mindsets?

Scripture or Quote to Meditate On or Consider:

I'm grateful for:

____

____

____

____

I'm challenged by:

____

____

____

____

Action Steps

○

○

○

Reflections On This Month

My Accomplishments This Month:

____

____

____

____

Where Did I Fall Short In Meeting A Challenge?

____

____

____

____

What Adjustments Can I Make to Move Forward?

____

____

____

____

Goals Tracker

My Top Goals(s) For This Quarter	
1	
2	
3	

To Do List

....

....

....

....

....

Action Plan

STEP 5

STEP 4

STEP 3

STEP 2

STEP 1

Rewards	1	2	3	4

Month 4: _______________

What goal will I set for this month?

____

____

____

____

____

____

What words or mindsets might hinder me from meeting my goal?

____

____

____

____

____

____

____

How will I "rewrite the script" to reflect new words and mindsets?

____

____

____

____

____

____

____

Scripture or Quote to Meditate On or Consider:

I'm grateful for:

____

____

____

____

I'm challenged by:

____

____

____

____

Action Steps

○ ____________________________

○ ____________________________

○ ____________________________

Reflections On This Month

My Accomplishments This Month:

____

____

____

____

____

Where Did I Fall Short In Meeting A Challenge?

____

____

____

____

____

What Adjustments Can I Make to Move Forward?

____

____

____

____

____

Month 5: ______________

What goal will I set for this month?

What words or mindsets might hinder me from meeting my goal?

How will I "rewrite the script" to reflect new words and mindsets?

____

____

____

____

____

____

____

Scripture or Quote to Meditate On or Consider:

I'm grateful for:

____

____

____

____

I'm challenged by:

____

____

____

____

Action Steps

○

○

○

Reflections On This Month

My Accomplishments This Month:

____

____

____

____

____

Where Did I Fall Short In Meeting A Challenge?

____

____

____

____

____

What Adjustments Can I Make to Move Forward?

____

____

____

____

____

Month 6: ______________

What goal will I set for this month?

____

____

____

____

____

____

____

What words or mindsets might hinder me from meeting my goal?

____

____

____

____

____

____

____

How will I "rewrite the script" to reflect new words and mindsets?

____

____

____

____

____

____

Scripture or Quote to Meditate On or Consider:

I'm grateful for:

____

____

____

____

I'm challenged by:

____

____

____

____

Action Steps

Reflections On This Month

My Accomplishments This Month:

____

____

____

____

Where Did I Fall Short In Meeting A Challenge?

____

____

____

____

What Adjustments Can I Make to Move Forward?

____

____

____

____

Goals Tracker

My Top Goal(s) For This Quarter
1
2
3

To Do List

Action Plan

STEP 1

STEP 2

STEP 3

STEP 4

STEP 5

Rewards	1	2	3	4

Month 7: _______________

What goal will I set for this month?

____

____

____

____

____

____

____

What words or mindsets might hinder me from meeting my goal?

____

____

____

____

____

____

How will I "rewrite the script" to reflect new words and mindsets?

Scripture or Quote to Meditate On or Consider:

I'm grateful for:

____

____

____

____

I'm challenged by:

____

____

____

____

Action Steps

○

○

○

Reflections On This Month

My Accomplishments This Month:

____

____

____

____

____

Where Did I Fall Short In Meeting A Challenge?

____

____

____

____

What Adjustments Can I Make to Move Forward?

____

____

____

____

Month 8: ________________

What goal will I set for this month?

____

____

____

____

____

____

____

What words or mindsets might hinder me from meeting my goal?

____

____

____

____

____

____

____

How will I "rewrite the script" to reflect new words and mindsets?

____

____

____

____

____

____

Scripture or Quote to Meditate On or Consider:

I'm grateful for:

____

____

____

____

I'm challenged by:

____

____

____

____

Action Steps

○

○

○

Reflections On This Month

My Accomplishments This Month:

____

____

____

____

Where Did I Fall Short In Meeting A Challenge?

____

____

____

____

What Adjustments Can I Make to Move Forward?

____

____

____

____

Month 9: ______________

What goal will I set for this month?

____

____

____

____

____

____

What words or mindsets might hinder me from meeting my goal?

____

____

____

____

____

____

How will I "rewrite the script" to reflect new words and mindsets?

____

____

____

____

____

____

____

Scripture or Quote to Meditate On or Consider:

I'm grateful for:

____

____

____

____

I'm challenged by:

____

____

____

____

Action Steps

- ○
- ○
- ○

Reflections On This Month

My Accomplishments This Month:

____

____

____

____

____

Where Did I Fall Short In Meeting A Challenge?

____

____

____

____

What Adjustments Can I Make to Move Forward?

____

____

____

____

Goals Tracker

My Top Goal(s) For This Quarter
1
2
3

To Do List

....
....
....
....
....

Action Plan

STEP 1
STEP 2
STEP 3
STEP 4
STEP 5

Rewards	1	2	3	4

Month 10: _______________

What goal will I set for this month?

____

____

____

____

____

____

____

What words or mindsets might hinder me from meeting my goal?

____

____

____

____

____

____

____

How will I "rewrite the script" to reflect new words and mindsets?

____

____

____

____

____

____

Scripture or Quote to Meditate On or Consider:

I'm grateful for:

____

____

____

____

I'm challenged by:

____

____

____

____

Action Steps

○

○

○

Reflections On This Month

My Accomplishments This Month:

____

____

____

____

Where Did I Fall Short In Meeting A Challenge?

____

____

____

____

What Adjustments Can I Make to Move Forward?

____

____

____

____

Month 11: _________________

What goal will I set for this month?

____

____

____

____

____

____

____

What words or mindsets might hinder me from meeting my goal?

____

____

____

____

____

____

____

How will I "rewrite the script" to reflect new words and mindsets?

____

____

____

____

____

____

____

Scripture or Quote to Meditate On or Consider:

I'm grateful for:

____

____

____

____

I'm challenged by:

____

____

____

____

Action Steps

○

○

○

Reflections On This Month

My Accomplishments This Month:

____

____

____

____

Where Did I Fall Short In Meeting A Challenge?

____

____

____

____

What Adjustments Can I Make to Move Forward?

____

____

____

____

Month 12: _______________

Reflections

____

____

____

____

____

____

____

Where has my mindset changed and how?

____

____

____

____

____

____

What practices (actions) have I changed this year?

____

____

____

____

____

____

____

Scripture or Quote that has been meaningful to my journey:

I'm grateful for:

____

____

____

____

I'm challenged by:

____

____

____

____

Action Steps

○ ____________________________

○ ____________________________

○ ____________________________

This year I am most grateful for:

____

____

____

____

____

____

____

The new possibilities I have discovered within myself:

____

____

____

____

____

____

____

Where is my inner compass pointing now?

____

____

____

____

____

____

____

What am I going to do with what I know?

____

____

____

____

____

____

____

____